ALL I NEED IS ME

7 STEPS
TO POSITIVE
SELF ESTEEM

Anthony Phillips

Anthony Phillips

7 Steps To Positive Self Esteem
Copyright © 2008
Anthony L. Phillips

ALL RIGHTS RESERVED

Unless otherwise indicated, all Scripture quotations are
taken from the King James Version of the Bible.

ISBN-978-0-6152659-8-8
Second printing (2/2012)

For Information contact:
Anthony Phillips
info@amphillips.com
www.amphillips.com

Dedication

This book is dedicated to the young men and women that are seeking to improve their self esteem and haven't found the inspiration or motivation to do so. I hope that you will take these 7 steps to becoming all that God has planned for you. I truly believe that you are one of tomorrow's leaders! Nothing or no one from this day forward will be able to stop you from reaching your destiny. Where you are today is just the first chapter in the book you will someday write to inspire others.

Acknowledgements

There are a number of people that I would like to thank for the inspiration and support in the past years leading up to this first of many books to come.

My first acknowledgement is to **God** and to our **Lord & Savior Jesus Christ**. Without his grace, this would not have been possible. We give God the glory in all that we do.

My mother, **Dorothy Luckey**, has inspired me in more ways than she realizes. Being a single parent mother rearing 3 boys and working two jobs, yet we never wanted for anything. Thank you for all that you have done for me and my wife.

My children, **Anthony, Rhyne and Jordan** have been the motivation behind this book.

My **Aunt Ethel**, although you raised five children of your own, you always had a little extra in you for me and my two brothers. God bless you!

Acknowledgements

My two elder brothers, **Stanley and Royal**, taught me how to stand up for myself and instilled in me the attributes of what it takes to be a man.

Daniel Blanks, Darryl Williams and David Miller have been true friends and provided me with support, correction and inspiration that I needed from real friends. My foundation began with each of these men and my house remains unmovable because of them.

Vicki Hallman & Karen Marshall, my friends that have been by my side from day one!

Last but not least, **Dion Jordan**, who helped me to bring this dream to fruition! I truly understand what you mean by All That It Takes Is All That You've Got - And All That You've Got Is All That It Takes! God bless you for teaching me how to live our dream.
www.dionjordan.com

Anthony Phillips

TABLE OF CONTENTS

Seven Steps to Positive Self-Esteem

Anthony Phillips

INTRODUCTION

What is Self Esteem?

Do you truly love yourself? Chances are; there may be a few things you don't like about you. Everyone has a natural dislike for certain traits they have to live with everyday. You are no exception.

It may sound vain to love oneself. Look around and you'll see people every day who seem to love themselves too much. You'll see girls who wear too much makeup or guys who strut and flex their muscles like 50 Cent. It's almost considered a bad thing these days to love yourself. Society has trained people to find fault with each other. People have become very judgmental; especially teenagers. They sometimes huddle together in cliques and point or laugh at kids who are easy targets. Maybe you have been in a group of teens and seen this type of behavior with your own eyes. Maybe you've even been one of the kids that the others pointed at. The mean words people say can cause serious damage to one's self esteem.

It can leave you wondering –

- Am I good looking enough?
- Am I smart enough?
- What am I good at?
- Is my appearance okay?
- What if no one likes me?

Teens often go out of their way to be liked. A small pimple can ruin your whole day, if you let it. Rest assured; things that seem so big and important to you right now will one day pale in comparison to the large realities of adulthood. One day you will look back to your teen years with fondness and cherished memories. Half of the things that seem like such catastrophes at the moment will only be something to laugh about later.

You will one day arrive at your class reunion and run into a classmate you have not seen since graduation. *"Remember that time you had stage fright in front of the whole school?"* you might reminisce. Right now, if something truly embarrassing happened to you, would you be able to laugh it off or would you let it affect your sense of self worth?

That is exactly what self esteem is. The meaning refers to an individual's sense of value. It is the question we all ask ourselves at some point; "What is my worth to my family, coach, friends or teachers?" Self-esteem refers to the extent that a person approves of oneself.

As a common term, self esteem is used to describe how someone feels about who they are. Ask yourself the following self-reflections:

- Do you feel like you are contributing something worthwhile to this life?
- Do you feel that you are a good person?
- Do you like to give more than receive?
- Are you happy with yourself?
- Do you like the way you look?

Don't worry... nobody will be looking at your answers. These are merely questions to determine whether you feel that you have a high self esteem or a low self esteem. This is not a test!

People with high self-esteem:

- Are confident.
- Are willing and able to communicate their needs to others without fear of saying how they truly feel.
- Experience very little shame when placed in an uncomfortable situation.
- Focus on the good, rather than the negative aspects of life.
- Focus on having social, family, financial, health and educational needs met.
- Have happy and healthy friendships. With normal people (as normal as they can be).
- Reach out to motivate others.
- Stick up for people, even when others falter or poke fun at them.
- Don't always go along with everyone else if it's the wrong thing to do.
- Make decisions with honesty and integrity.
- Are leaders more often than followers.
- Seek out necessities for survival.

- Can admit their individual human limitations, strengths and weaknesses.

Self-doubt and fear are the biggest reasons for low self esteem. At an early age, very often kids are told repeatedly of what they can't do. But remember – adults are not always right. Your own parents and teachers were raised by their parents and teachers. Unless someone told them any differently, the same values and attitudes will be passed down.

Of course, this book is not intended to plant any amount of disrespect towards the people who are raising you, loving you and taking care of you. Rather, it is a challenge to open your eyes to the wonder of you.

When people tell you not to do something for your own good, you should sit up and listen; however, when they say you can't do something because of

a) Incapability;

b) Lack of resources;

c) Disbelief of your skills;

d) Selfishness;

none of these are reasons that should hold you back from becoming who you are meant to be.

As an example, I knew a lady at church who had a nice husband and two beautiful daughters. They were a happy family to anyone who knew them. Upon talking to her one day, I learned that she had been born with several birth defects. "I only had one eye and my nose was twice the size it was supposed to be," she described herself. "Throughout elementary and junior high school I was painfully shy and often made fun of. Even after the surgery to fix my face, I was never very sociable in high school and I cried about how ugly I was every day."

The lady went on to describe how her parents had made her feel worthless because of the defects. Her father had been an alcoholic and her mother was bitter. "No man will ever want to marry you," they told her. She believed it and subsequently had a very low self-worth throughout her childhood and teen years.
She had few friends and was shy because she lacked the confidence to talk to people.

College life was better away from home. After college, she met a man at work who complimented her umbrella and they fell in love. They had two beautiful daughters and lived a very happy life. Had she listened to the negativity of her parents, she may have lived a life of despair. But instead, she followed her true path and found a great husband and wonderful life.

It can be the hardest thing to remain positive when you are surrounded by negative people. Most of that challenge lies in the ability to overcome the self-defeating behavior and thoughts that can be brought about by other people. Not just family – but friends, acquaintances and adults sometimes slap their own insecurities on each other unintentionally because they are afraid of failing themselves.

People with low self-esteem:

- Lack confidence.
- Can't express themselves when faced with challenges and tough situations.
- Suffer from failure on most ventures because they lack the drive to follow through to completion.
- Are not aware of their true talents and skills.
- Seem like lost souls who are naturally unhappy.
- Usually have less love, attention or good parenting skills.

15

- Sometimes come from bad or dysfunctional families.
- Make fun of other people a lot to hide their own insecurities.
- Judge others' clothing, appearances or situations to make themselves feel better.

"Let nothing be done through strife or vainglory;
but in lowliness of mind let each esteem the other better
than themselves."
~Philippians 2:3~

Having a good self-esteem is a quality that can be learned. The good news is that anyone can learn, at any age. With some simple practice tools, you can take baby steps to positive self improvement. The beauty of this journey is that you can only have positive results. Don't be discouraged if you're not happy about where you are right now. Keep reading, because you're about to feel much better about yourself and you will notice your self-esteem increasing after reading this book!

STEP ONE

SELF-ACCEPTANCE

Sonya was the most popular kid at school. She had beautiful, curly black hair and standout eyes with long lashes. She had perfect white teeth and natural beauty, even with very little makeup. Her tiny little cheerleader body was perfectly proportioned and everywhere she went, people fawned all over her. She wore fashionable clothes that other girls at school tried to copy. Sonya was a trendsetter; yet inside, Sonya was unhappy. She did things for attention as a rebellious way to cover up her own unhappiness. For example, Sonya wore very short skirts and flirted provocatively with older boys. She flaunted her womanhood, although she was just a young girl. Unfortunately, her low self-esteem made her a target for predators.

One night at dusk, Sonya began to walk less than half a mile home from her friend's house. Her tight sweater did little to protect her from the chill. She heard footsteps behind her. They were solid, hard steps; unmistakably that of a man's. She walked faster and so did the steps. Sonya started to run. Her home was within sight, but she dodged into her neighbor's driveway and banged on the door. Fortunately, the neighbor answered just in time for Sonya to turn and see the man turn back into the dark, defeated.

Sonya nearly missed a potentially terrible situation. Her lack of self-confidence had caused her to be careless. She thought she needed to dress sexy to be liked, drawing attention to her physical appearance. The desire to look attractive to the opposite sex is often misused by teenagers. It can lead to dangerous consequences.

Movie stars and celebrities wear scanty outfits; therefore teenagers who idolize their favorite actresses think they must dress that way in order to attract attention. Young people who wear next to nothing are sometimes lacking self confidence. They feel a need to dress like the stars they see on TV in order to belong.

Stand apart from the crowd by incorporating a stylish, yet modest blend of your own cool ideas. It's okay to browse through magazines to keep up with trends, but ideally you are an individual and should learn to dress and behave in a classy way. People as a society have more respect for men and women who don't overtly show off in public. Very often, people who dress and behave in a way that brings attention do so because they have a low self worth and believe that they need to go over-the-top in order to impress and be accepted by their peers, pals and society. Remember, your body is a temple. You demonstrate how you feel about yourself by how well you nurture, respect and care for yourself.

Self Acceptance:

Each living thing on earth has a purpose and a place in the ecology of nature and mankind. God has a purpose for you – from the top of your head to the bottom of your feet. You are created of the divine energy of God and the great Universe.

When you accept yourself, you are able to concentrate on your positive qualities and consider what needs to be improved. Self-acceptance is when you appreciate your own unique God-given talents, gifts and characteristics. Yes, that even includes your freckles, curly hair, pretty eyes and funny sense of humor.

Be realistic about your talents and skills. Ask yourself what you're good at. Everyone has natural ability. You could be the best basketball player on the team; or the best artist in your class; or the fastest computer whiz. What can you do to put your best foot forward and offer your skills to others? Happiness comes from accepting both your positive and negative qualities.

Remember these 12 ACCEPTANCE PRINCIPLES:

1) In this world, at least twelve people love you.
2) Your smile will bring joy and happiness to people, even strangers or people who dislike you.
3) Someone thinks about you or dreams about you every night as they lie in bed.
4) There's at least one person in the whole world that you would do absolutely anything for.
5) You are unlike anyone else – you are most unique.
6) There is someone you don't even know about in the world that loves you right now.
7) Hang on to every compliment you receive and be rid of any rude remarks.

8) Nobody would ever have reason to hate you, unless they were jealous and wished they could be just like you.

9) You mean the whole world to at least one person.

10) Be a loving friend to everyone, even those who do you wrong. Doing good will come back to you one day.

11) Even when you make the biggest mistake ever, something good will come from it.

12) When you feel like the world has turned its back on you, keep going and look straight ahead.

Accepting your own self and including those traits that you may see as flaws, is a true beginning to acquiring a renewed sense of confidence and self-esteem. It can be difficult to look in the mirror each day without finding something to criticize in the reflection that returns your gaze.

Instead of finding fault with yourself, try giving your reflection some positive words. It feels weird to talk to yourself in the mirror, but it may just make you smile. Start with simple phrases like:

"I am going to have a good day today."

"I'm not going to let anyone or anything bother me."

21

"I am ready to succeed."

"My eyes are really nice, if I do say so myself."

If you'd rather avoid talking to yourself in the first person, you can reword it as if you are talking to a good friend. It goes something like this:

"You look beautiful today. That outfit makes you look good."

"You will not let anyone bring you down today and you will be able to handle any situation that happens."

"You are unstoppable."

As funny as it may seem, talking to yourself in the mirror is very constructive. Once you do it a few times, you might actually look forward to it. It is the ultimate way to truly accept who you are.

Look at your own eyes, smile, hair and clothes. Those are only physical qualities, but as a teenager they are always high on the priority list of importance; however, physical appearances change over time. People grow out of those "weird" puberty stages. Physical characteristics are not what matter in the grand scheme of your life. They are most important when you are a teen.

Let's face it, school is tough and kids are very critical of each other. If someone calls you a name that is offensive, most of the time they are doing so because of their own low self-esteem. Maybe you could introduce them to this book.

On the other hand, it is a bad habit of humans in general to judge and poke fun at other people. Please, be the bigger person. Once you accept yourself and realize that words people say can no longer affect you in any way, then you will be on a path to self-discovery. You will not ever reach the end of this path... it is a long journey that will take up most of your life.

Surround yourself with positive friends who don't belittle people just to make themselves more popular. Popularity is not a contest, although it may seem that way. You can be cool AND still be accepted by other teens, even when you don't join in or participate in their cruel words to other kids. Honestly, are those the kinds of friends you want, anyway? Miserable people like to make everyone around them miserable.

Looks are only on the surface. Next time someone in your group of friends says something mean to a fellow classmate, simply say – "Hey, c'mon – that's really not cool." Chances are, by taking the initiative to stick up for someone who isn't as perfect as your classmates think they are, they will respect you more for saying something. You are not willing to stand by and let others be ridiculed; therefore, you will be deemed as friend to everyone. It's better to have friends in life, that's for sure.

Foul words sting for a long time, but kind deeds will be fondly remembered for a lifetime. Even if you never see some of these kids you are surrounded by right now after graduation; they will remember who was nice or who was a bully.

The ironic part is that by the time you get to your first class reunion (usually ten years following graduation); the people who were the best-looking in High School are often very different when you see them in adulthood. Very often those "jocks" and "cheerleaders" or prom kings and queens have already changed drastically by the time a 10 or 20 year reunion takes place. Some men will lose their hair. Some girls may have a family one day and have a harder time keeping shapely bodies. It doesn't really matter in the grand scheme of things.

What matters most is who you are as a person and who you surround yourself with.

Set an example of kindness by going against the rotten words used against fellow classmates. Next time you hear a mean lash by a good friend of yours that is targeted toward someone who is "different" or unaccepted, don't just stand by and say nothing. You will gain more respect by speaking your mind.

A positive self esteem equals confidence. You are not afraid to be assertive. Try these confidence boosters:

APPLY THESE 7 CONFIDENCE BOOSTERS:

1) Pay yourself at least one compliment every day. Say it out loud in the mirror.

2) Give someone you don't like at least one compliment today. Choose at least one person each day to consciously say a positive phrase to.

3) When you overhear a fellow student or friend make fun of someone else, speak up and don't allow it.

4) Work on your own issues and avoid involving yourself in everyone else's drama.

5) Next time someone says something mean to you, smile and thank them for bringing it to your attention. Then tell them to have a great day. This will throw people off and make them less likely to repeat offensive words to you in the future.

6) Let nothing phase you. If something goes wrong, just shrug and say, "Oh well, I am doing my best."

7) Before bed every night, be thankful for at least one thing that happened to you today. If you have more than one thing, give thanks for everything.

Who you are right now is not who you will be in a few years. Well, let's clarify that. You are creating who you *will be, right now!* You are like an artist, creating a beautiful canvas painting that will one day be good enough to hang in galleries. Bring only those favorite qualities with you as you move onward toward your destiny.

So, what happens if family is the cause of your grievances? Some teens have the misfortune of a not-so-ideal home life. Kids these days often have to live out of backpacks, swapping from Mom's house to Dad's house to accommodate divorced parents. The intertwining of families can wreak havoc on a teen's schedule and self-esteem. Some kids end up with mean stepbrothers and sisters, or problems with parents, grandparents or other family members. No one has a perfect life, so do your best to get along with everyone despite the circumstances.

While you may not fall into that category, it is important not to let your parents or siblings, or any other family member devalue your own self worth. You can respect the difference in opinions of others without it affecting your own mental well-being. In other words, if your own family says something to offend you, do not let it bring down your spirit, nor your positive attitude.

Here's an example:

Daniel was a great athlete. He was a receiver on his high school's football team and was also a pretty good student, with mostly B's and a few A's on his report card. When his parents got divorced the year prior to his freshman year, he acted like it was no big deal. But on the inside, Daniel was sad and disappointed.

When his parents had been married, they rarely missed a game. His father usually drove him to practice and was a huge advocate of his playing sports. Although his parents didn't get along very well, Daniel never thought they would actually split up. He was confused and hurt; even though his mother explained that it wasn't his fault and had nothing to do with how either of them felt about their son.

Daniel continued on, but his grades took a slight dip in the last semester. He made the JV football team as a starter, but Daniel developed a "chip on his shoulder" attitude. He seemed cross most of the time and slammed things around. He yelled at people for petty things. Worst of all, Daniel began hanging around a few rebellious kids who were considered misfits in most social circles.

He stayed with his father most weekends, but when his father got a new girlfriend after the divorce, Daniel was less than pleased with his choice. To top it off, his Dad started coming late to Daniel's football games and missed a few of them altogether.

Secretly, Daniel was terribly bummed out by his father's absence to his football games. He had been such a big fan and believer, always encouraging Daniel to play his best. Without his Dad there, what was the point?

Some of Daniel's new friends were bad influences. When they fired up a joint one day and passed it to Daniel, he willingly took a few puffs. He began smoking it more and more frequently after the first time. He was late for practice twice and was winded whenever the coach made the team do sprints and field exercises. Daniel developed an attitude to which he didn't care anymore. His self-esteem was low, although he didn't realize it.

Only bad things happen when you surround yourself with bad influences. People are not bad; it is who they become when they have a low self-worth that is disturbing. When people lack confidence, they have a tendency to "follow the crowd" and succumb to peer pressure. They want to feel liked. They want to belong to something bigger to feel acceptance. Teens are especially influential. Some feel betrayed by a parent, sibling or family member and it leads to costly mistakes.

Daniel's mistake was in hanging out with the bad boys and trying marijuana. It cost him a position on the football team. Random urine tests are used to make sure athletes are clean. Since Daniel's performance was also lagging, the two things combined caused him to be cut from the team. Daniel could have gone on to receive a college scholarship because his athletic ability was that good. Instead, his low self-worth caused him to seek negative influences. The sad part is that in the end, he was only hurting himself and his own future.

Always Remember This:

- ONLY BAD THINGS WILL HAPPEN WHEN YOU HANG OUT WITH BAD INFLUENCES.
- YOU NEVER NEED TO "FOLLOW THE CROWD" TO BELONG. YOU CAN STAND ON YOUR OWN TWO FEET.
- EMBRACE AND USE YOUR TALENTS, EVEN IF A PARENT OR SOMEONE CLOSE TO YOU DOES LET YOU DOWN.
- NEGATIVE BEHAVIOR OF OTHER PEOPLE IS NOT YOUR FAULT.

Of course, Daniel's father didn't intentionally cause his son's lack of confidence. Daniel needed to accept himself and the fact that his parents could not be there for him in the same way as before the divorce. It didn't mean they didn't love him as much, even if in Daniel's mind it seemed as if his Dad didn't care. By not going to his games or taking an interest, his Dad was mistakenly sending a signal that Daniel's talents no longer mattered; therefore, why bother?

Not so. If you love to do something, you should love it just as much whether anyone is there to appreciate it or not. These are *your* gifts and talents that God gave you, whether it's to be a tennis champion, photographer for the yearbook, lead actor in a school play, captain of the cheering squad or the high school mascot. You don't need approval to do things that give you joy. Accept the true purpose behind these talents, because each talent that you possess now is a step in what you are meant to become.

STEP TWO

RESILIENCE

You may have heard the word resilience before. It's a cute word of French heritage – pronounced:

re·sil·ience ◀)   \ri-'zil-yən(t)s\

The true meaning of resilience is to have an ability to bounce back or adjust easily from misfortune, mistakes or changes as they come. The French used it to describe leaping back from being stretched or compressed. Let's think about that for a second.

Every day, certain things may happen to you that are undesirable. It could be as simple as losing one of your belongings such as a wallet or purse. Do you roll with the punches, or do you wallow in self-pity? Do you brush it off, or do you yell and react with anger?

Life's challenges are not ganging up on you. It may seem like it sometimes, when bad things compound on top of each other and your emotions take over. At times you may wonder, "Why do bad things always seem to happen to me?" Yet, that is not the way it truly is.

Later on you will learn that bad things often stem from one or two original decisions and actions that were made. You've probably heard the old expression, '*When it rains, it pours.*'

Having difficulties in your personal relationships, academics or finances may make you feel at times like you have been stretched and pulled to a breaking point, just as the French term describes.

Right now it may seem like the demands of your youthfulness are piled high. You have so many people who have high expectations of you, right?

The fact is... you are much stronger spiritually and mentally than you might think. You have the ability to overcome great obstacles, challenges and mistakes. When bad things happen, it is not the end of the world. It may be major or minor, but just do your best to brace yourself for the consequences. Go forward with integrity, which is having a quality of high morals.

From this moment on, try to look at each situation and take it at face value. "It is what it is." You can't do anything at the moment to change some things that happen. When someone wrongs you, or when someone you love gets hurt, or you fail a test, it is natural to lament and feel down. Choosing to move forward in a spirit of positive energy will make the situation far more tolerable than flipping out and becoming angry.

"Put on the full armor of God so that you can take your stand against the devil's schemes."
~ Ephesians 6:11 (NIV) ~

It's easier said than done, isn't it? Human beings are naturally emotional and have feelings to sift through. Anger, disappointment and despair are natural emotions that everyone will experience. Maybe the reason is to appreciate those great moments in between.

No one has a perfect life. No one expects you not to feel pain or sorrow sometimes. Life is meant to be enjoyed through all of its ups and downs. How you deal with the issues that come about will be important in the decisions you make in the future. You can choose to move forward and make the best decisions that are available to you.

'That's all fine and dandy,' you might be thinking, *'but what does resilience have to do with my self-esteem?'* A lot!

When you are resilient, you have a positive 'can-do' attitude, which gives you more energy to be able to stand up and try again. Resilience is uplifting. Rather than feeling defeated, you will feel hopeful in anticipation of something better. A person who is self-resilient has all of the mental willpower to put up a good fight toward what they know to be right and good. Resilient people feel that life is basically fair, but not without some challenges that must be overcome.

Otherwise, the only alternative is defeat. Defeat turns people into victims. Victims believe that they are being 'singled out' by God or by the world around them. They believe that they are bad luck charms or that they have no control over what happens to them. They wish away their lives and purposefully make poor decisions in order to maintain the self-dejectedness. It's a terrible habit that is often learned by an adult and is ingrained by an early age. Some teens are just prone to feeling defeated because of lack of self-esteem.

Either way, at this stage in your life it is far from being a lost battle. You are just beginning your journey. Take these two ladies, for example:

Michelle and Rhyne were paired up at the dinner table of a Christmas party with their husbands, who were co-workers at the same company. As the men went off to mingle, the two ladies struck up a conversation.

It was learned sometime within the conversation that Michelle owned a travel agency, affording herself and her family the opportunity to go on frequent vacations. While still young, Michelle had become very successful with her business and was able to afford nice clothes, hair, jewelry and a personal trainer. Rhyne, who was middle-aged, was more subdued and less flashy. She had a grumpy look on her face most of the time, and while Michelle was always cheerful and smiling, Rhyne was clearly upset about most everything she could find to point out.

She complained of not currently working due to a workman's comp claim, saying her back injury was causing her great pain and misfortune both financially and otherwise. Her health had suffered, as well as her relationship with her husband. She pointed at other guests throughout the evening, saying not-so-nice things under her breath. Rhyne was basically a miserable lady who had probably lived most of her life that way.

Michelle, on the other hand, had started her business during the very ripe age of her mid-twenties. Her husband came along a couple of years later, and they fell in love and had a handsome son.

"It must be nice to have the perfect life," Rhyne said sarcastically. "I've had a hard life. Bad things always happen to me somehow."

"Well, it must be terrible to go through life like that," Michelle said apologetically.

"So, you're a travel agent, huh? Where have you been to?" asked Rhyne.

"Europe, Venezuela, Hawaii, California..."

Rhyne interrupted. "I always wanted to go to Ireland but it's too late for that now."

"Why is it too late? You're still alive, aren't you?" Michelle questioned.

"Oh, I'm too old for that now," sighed Rhyne. "Besides, my husband would never want to go."

"How do you know? Maybe he would if you asked him. Don't assume he won't," said Michelle. "Tell him how much it would mean to you."

Rhyne appeared to be skeptical. "So, how'd you get your own travel business, anyway? You must have had to go to college a long time or have Daddy's money."

Michelle smiled. "No, I worked for a travel agency after college and then started my own company. It was always a dream of mine to do it because I love to see different cultures all over the world. My father was a welder. He worked hard but I was not born with a silver spoon."

Rhyne looked jealous, but curious. "I had a hard life. I could never do anything like that. I didn't have a chance to go to college."

"Actually, my life wasn't so easy growing up either. My Dad and I lost my mother when I was only 11. We had to work hard to make it. I had to take on a lot of household responsibilities for us to get by," said Michelle. She went on. "My major in college has nothing to do with the travel agency. I just learned when I got the job at the travel place and happened to be good at it! I actually have an Associate's Degree as a paralegal".

"Well isn't that great. Good for you," Rhyne said sarcastically.

The difference between these two ladies is that although both had difficulties through life, one chose to become a *victim*, while the other chose to become *victorious*. The victim just watches bad things happen and complains about it, feeling defeated. The victorious one moves on from certain challenges, almost propelled by overcoming them. Victims think they have no control – vs. victorious people who take control over their adversities (challenges) and find a way to turn them around.

Switching from a victim mentality to one of victory will be a step in your progress toward positive self-esteem. Start by seeing difficulties as hurdles and pretend you are a track star who has to jump over them to reach the finish line. With God's help, you can overcome frustrating limitations knowing that He "has your back".

Part of resilience and bouncing back from any situation is to let go of it once it has been conquered. Adults sometimes refer to past mistakes as "baggage". Baggage is the problems that you carry with you throughout your life. When you carry baggage with you into the next day, week, years, or beyond – your spirit becomes tainted. Resilience is letting go of baggage that binds you. Leave the baggage right where it belongs, in the past. Baggage is heavy, cumbersome and generally just a pain to have.

What are some examples of baggage?

- Past hurts.
- Bitterness toward relationships that have gone sour.
- Anger towards parents or people who raised you.
- Regrets.
- Resentment (secretly feeling mad at someone without letting that person know).
- Excuses & Problems of any kind.

Drop your baggage off today. It may feel like a great weight has been lifted off your back. Why are you carrying around all of that extra weight, anyway? It will feel so good to rid yourself of past hurts and disappointments.

You see, baggage will turn you into a victim. The more of those negative qualities that you hang on to and bring with you throughout your life, the more likely you are to become a victim. Baggage becomes a heavy load to your spirit.

It is a long, slow and painful journey to carry baggage with you. Baggage will inhibit your freedom. Let it go and be rid of unnecessary strife in your life. Your personal well-being does depend on a happy spirit.

"Let go [of your concerns] and Let God;
Then you will know that I am God.
I rule the nations. I rule the earth."
~ Psalm 46:10 ~

Are there any areas of your life that you realize need to be changed? You can bounce back from all of those hurts once you realize that God is behind the wheel of your life. You are just a passenger. He will direct you where you need to go if you just ride along beside him in trust and faith.

This does not mean that everything bad will magically disappear. Life is rarely that simple. What you can count on is that life will continue to present you with events that you may not always enjoy. Yet, with self-resilience, you will become confident in your own ability to make the best decisions possible for a better outcome. Amazingly, by shedding all of your past hurts, regrets, and anger and by handling situations as they arise – your resilience will give you just the confidence you need.

STEP THREE

HONESTY

What does honesty have to do with your self-esteem? Honesty is defined as an ability to act with integrity and truth. A person that is honest about every aspect of his or her life can improve their self-esteem. By taking a closer look at their true capabilities and talents, they can accurately decide where their time and energy will best be spent. They can focus on their true purpose, which creates more confidence.

"If one can actually revert to the truth, then a great deal of one's suffering can be erased; because a great deal of suffering is based on sheer lies."

~ R.D. Lang ~

When you are honest about the most obvious areas of your life – like school, friends, family, homework, chores, church and sports; then you can focus on determining the areas that most need to be strengthened. Take inventory of anything in your life that creates discomfort for you. You can pinpoint one specific thing that causes you the most grief, or several things that bother you the most. It could be your looks, peer pressure, not enough time, poor choices in friends, a fear of speaking in public, bad grades, or anything you deem as bothersome. Anything on your list should be a new focus for change. Rather than dwelling on the negative, you can use this honesty assessment as a foundation to move forward.

You have already learned about resilience. So, now you can be honest with yourself in realizing exactly what things are causing you the most grief.

Here's how to tackle those areas that you have identified. If it's your looks that bring you discomfort, then you must determine what it would take to change. You have already learned about self-acceptance, so now it's time to learn about honesty.

Maybe you are overweight, which is something that can be changed. Honesty allows you to go to the heart of the matter. Then, you can address the problem and make positive motion towards becoming the confident and best YOU that you truly deserve to be.

Maybe you lack the education you need. Maybe you're not as good at sports as other kids, yet you desperately want to try out for the team. Instead of feeling like you have no control; just be honest about your own imperfections. Imperfections are those things that only YOU deem as imperfect. God doesn't see you the same way you do. These are only challenges, not setbacks.

Most of the time, we identify the areas that need improvement but fail to do what is necessary to overcome them. We make up excuses. We tell ourselves we can't do it. That is where the lack of self-esteem comes into play.

Stop procrastinating! It's time to make a difference in your own life. Be honest about your flaws, as they will only make you better as you overcome them. You can lose weight if you want to. You can study harder to become smarter. You can get better at sports through practice, over and over – even if some of the other kids are naturally better than you. We all have individual aptitudes that are like no one else on the planet. Not using them is a shame.

There was a kid named Tony at school, who was often made fun of because of the clothes he wore and the way he looked. He wore the same two shirts and rotated them every other day. His sneakers were well-worn and had holes in them. Tony was also kind of on the chubby side, had a little less hair on his mustache than some of the other teens and was a bit shy.

Tony allowed his appearance to be the cause of his low self-esteem. What the other kids did not know was that Tony's parents were struggling through very hard financial times. They were about to lose their home to a foreclosure. Things had been difficult since the auto manufacturer had lain off so many employees, including his father who had been working there for the past 15 years.

Every night, Tony busied himself with inventions. He was a natural born scientist and took miscellaneous parts from junky electronics that he had discovered and made very clever contraptions. Tony only had one close friend who lived about six telephone poles away on the same street. Sometimes he recruited his buddy to hold tools or test the inventions. The two had great fun doing it, although sometimes it was frustrating when the inventions didn't work.

Tony's friend said, "You will be a great inventor one day." It seemed like things were bleak for Tony and his family. Nevertheless, the encouragement and honesty of his friend kept Tony going.

One day he saw a contest online for the best invention. The winner would go to Chicago for the World's Fair. Tony instantly got a brainstorm for a new energy concept he had thought of. He would use whatever pieces he could find at the scrap yard, but others he didn't know how he would get because the parts were too expensive. His family's financial situation was not looking so good; nevertheless, Tony proceeded to start his invention.

One day his friend suggested he write letters to several big companies that had the components he would need to finish his invention. Surely some of these big companies would help a 15-year old boy? Tony hoped so.

With his friend's help, they mailed letters. It worked. Three companies sent boxes full of leftover plugs, wires and odds and ends that they no longer used. Tony was able to build an impressive creation with all of the miscellaneous scraps, plugs and parts that he had acquired.

Needless to say, he was invited to the World's Fair to compete against other kids from across the nation. His parents were proud. Tony came in first runner up in the entire nation for his energy concept. He was featured in the local newspaper. Some kids were indifferent about it, but many offered congratulations as he passed by in the hall.

After he graduated high school, Tony was offered a scholarship by a technical school. They had seen his design and were impressed. He went on to become an engineer and patented two of his ideas, which eventually put his income in the six-figure range.

The point of this story is that where you are right now is not where you may be in a very short amount of time. It doesn't matter what other people believe or think of you. It doesn't matter your financial status or looks. Be honest about your ability. If you know you have some special talent that no one else has, then just go forward and be productive. Ignore the naysayers.

No more focusing on failed accomplishments. The battle of the mind is where the enemy would like to keep you at all times, so let's not give him additional fuel by focusing on every negative thing you did wrong.

Having obstacles, whether they are financial, physical, and health, emotional or otherwise can make you feel like you will never be successful. You may not know quite yet what you are meant to do, but just keep going on your path to self-improvement, starting with personal evaluation and honesty.

"Pray for us; for we trust we have a good conscience, in all things willing to live honestly."

~ Hebrews 13:18 ~

Part of being honest with yourself is having courage to face your weaknesses. When you lack the courage to assert yourself in necessary situations or when faced with making a decision, you become reliant on other people to have the courage for you. In other words, you are a follower, rather than a leader. This is probably because you are unsure of yourself. You may even have a hard time interjecting your thoughts during a conversation, for fear of saying something wrong. You may be more comfortable letting other people make decisions on where to go and what to do in your circle of friends. Your lack of courage and assertiveness will make you a follower.

Once you identify what is holding you back, then you can determine the next step to move forward. Plan your future as a bold young person who is not afraid to speak your mind in a positive way.

"For kings, and for all that are in authority; that we may lead a quiet and peaceable life in all godliness and honesty."

~ Timothy 2:2 ~

This attention to true aptitude and skill will result in a higher level of success and a positive self-esteem. An honest person is not deceptive. By operating with honesty, courage and integrity you will be confident that you are always doing the right thing. You will make the best decisions that lead you on your true path and spiritual journey.

Anthony Phillips

STEP FOUR

ACCOUNTABILITY

To be held accountable is to take credit for your words and actions, both good and bad. By claiming them as your own, you become responsible for the outcome. You OWN it! Yes, that also includes the mistakes, for which there may be resulting punishments.

Not holding responsibility for all of your words and actions catches up with you. It is a sure path to low self esteem, confusion and serious consequences.

We learn from the example set forth by Eve:

"And the LORD God said unto the woman;
'What is this that thou have done?' And the woman said;
'The serpent beguiled me, and I did eat.'"
~ Genesis 3:13 ~

In the garden of Adam and Eve, her lack of accountability set a path for destruction and bewilderment that would be detrimental to all mankind. In essence, not claiming your words and actions is like pushing it off on someone else. Instead, you make excuses, lies and live a life of deceit. Even if what you have done (or not done) is just a mistake, step up to the plate and own it as yours. If you don't, someone innocent will end up taking the punishment for you. Are you going to let someone else pay for your mistakes? It would not be fair if it happened to you.

Lack of accountability might sound like this:

- "It wasn't me."
- "I didn't do it. Someone else did it."
- "I don't know what you're talking about."
- "Don't blame me."
- "I wasn't there."
- "I don't remember."
- "It's not my fault."

… and so on. We've all said things like these, defensively. We don't want to get in trouble or take the blame. A lack of accountability fuels perpetual excuses. Excuses are for people not interested in reality. Rather than taking the blame for anything, they push the blame to others or just deny it altogether. These people are "finger pointers". Inside, it may create a feeling of shamefulness, which is on the side of low self-worth.

"Excuses are tools of incompetence that build bridges to nowhere, and those who specialize in them seldom succeed in life."

~ *Author Unknown* ~

In the real world (you are on your way to the path of adulthood), people are judged for their productivity, or lack of it; therefore, a person that is accountable will strive to improve their current circumstances By Any Means Necessary! Complacency and laziness are not options for a responsible individual. Instead of relying on other people, to be accountable means to take action to better a situation.

You could use any number of examples. Here are a few to help you understand the relationship between accountability and self-esteem:

1) If you complain about the lack of money and have an unwillingness to work and earn it, you feel bad because you can't afford to buy nicer clothes.

You will ultimately feel more self-conscious; thus, creating a low self-esteem. Having a poor appearance contributes to a low self-worth. Someone who is accountable will go work to earn money. They will do whatever it takes – with confidence and conviction. A person who is accountable will try to make their own situation better through any way possible. Being accountable means to stand up and take action to better yourself.

2) Say, you break something at your house and try to cover it up. It gets discovered one day, but when you are questioned you blame your brother or sister. The sibling gets punished for your mistake, thus creating a feeling of shame on your part. Shame is associated with a low self-esteem. If you had fessed up when the accident first happened, your parents would not have been as angry because of your honesty.

3) You didn't prepare for a test and now you are nervous and afraid. Instead of studying, you were goofing off with your friends. Then to top it off, you didn't tell your teacher. So, you cheat and

copy from another student's paper. When questioned about it, you deny it and say it was a coincidence. The other student knows you cheated off her paper. Now she dislikes you because you cheated and then lied to the teacher. This can further add to low self-esteem and cause others to dislike you. By holding yourself accountable for not studying in the first place, you would own up to your mistake and admit your fault. In this example, one mistake led to several mistakes. If you think back to the many mistakes you have made, it can usually be pinpointed to one original decision that leads to many... like a snowball getting bigger and bigger until the problem becomes a disaster.

4) You know a couple who are dating, and you really have a crush on his or her significant other. To sabotage their breakup, you make up a story to one of their friends. Soon the story progresses into a huge rumor that spreads throughout the school. It ruins the love and happiness of the couple and breaks them up. One of them finds out that you were the source of the problem and

confronts you. You deny everything. The person is then shunned by other classmates. Inside, you feel guilt for your actions. Yet with no accountability for what you have done, another person's life and relationship can be ruined. Guilt and lack of integrity is associated with low self-esteem.

5) All of your friends have a MySpace account. Your parents said no when you asked for one. So, secretly you set up an account with a fake name. After a couple of months, your mother discovers the MySpace account and confronts you about it. Instead of being held accountable, you justify it by saying that all of your friends have one so you should too. Justifying negative actions has negative consequences. You may not understand why some kids have looser rules than you do, but follow the rules you are given and you will be rewarded. Who is to say why some horses have ten acres to graze, while others have a small pasture in the backyard? It may not be fair, but that is the pastures they were given. Your home is not like your friends' homes and your

family has a reason for their decisions. When your parents, teachers and authority figures see you making responsible choices, they will reward your actions with more independence later on when it really counts. There are reasons for their parenting requests, whether or not you may agree with them. Being accountable is to make conscious actions of goodness and living within the boundaries that you have. Freedom will come as a reward for responsibility.

While these are just a few scenarios, you surely could think of more examples of people who have let you down or failed you in some way. On the other side of it, there are probably people who you have let down at one time or another. It's all part of growing up. Right now, you have the tools you need to recharge your self-esteem by becoming accountable for your words and actions.

Think about a time that you had to rely on someone to accomplish something for you or come through for you. If they failed to complete the task, do you remember how you thought or felt about that person who lacked accountability to follow-through? Now... reverse the situation and place yourself in their shoes. It will help you to know how it feels to be on the other side of the fence.

People with low self-esteem become very defensive when they lack accountability. The defensiveness comes from fear – fear of getting caught, getting in trouble or losing a privilege. Defensive people become angry, but the reason is because of anger toward themselves and everyone around them. Defensive people can be very dangerous, because they believe the outside world is ganging up on them. The result of everything that happens is because of prior actions. Rather than having the viewpoint of evaluating self-behavior, defensive people act like victims. It's the POOR ME Syndrome!

To be accountable means to be responsible. Improve your self-esteem by being responsible with the tasks you were assigned. If you are a student, you must be responsible and diligent in your efforts to accomplish all work that is required of you. If you are a parent, you must be responsible for your children and care for them accordingly. If you are an employee, you must carry out the tasks and duties of your position to the best of your abilities.

There's another facet of this topic. Accountability also means to take action when you see a wrong done by someone else. For example, if you see someone vandalizing the school or neighbor's property, or a bully who is seriously threatening someone else, or you know of someone who shoplifts – these are all tests from God to see if you will step up to the plate and take action. You will never be wrong to tell someone when you see a wrong being done. If you prefer to do it anonymously, that is perfectly okay. You can call someone, tell parents, a teacher, principal or someone of authority that you know what is taking place but you prefer to remain anonymous. If you sit by and do nothing, then you could end up in a much worse situation. You could be blamed for it, or the behavior could keep continuing. Do you really want a bully beating up another kid? Are you going to turn your back when someone needs help? Part of having a high self-esteem is to have the confidence to rise and become a leader in any situation. Followers are the shy ones who hang back to avoid confrontation, that does no one any good and that is not who you are!

When you become an adult, the tests will continue, except on a larger scale. You'll be witness to many things both good and bad. You need to know what to do right now, as you are developing your adult mind and experiencing all of life's lessons. Next time your gut asks you, *'I wonder if I should say or do something'* when you see a bad deed going down – the answer is always yes. Of course, you shouldn't confuse this with putting yourself in any dangerous situation. There are several ways that each scenario could be handled and you are learning right now about decisions and choices. Lead your life in a God-like manner. That will always be the best choice.

Accountability is a tough practice to follow, because sometimes we just want to avoid any situation that involves a confrontation. Avoiding confrontation means you're unwilling to stand up and face the battle. It is another quality of low self-esteem, to be hiding behind the secrets that stem from bad behavior. Accountability also goes hand-in-hand with honesty, and with our forthcoming chapter of communication.

Unfortunately, confrontation is a fact of life. There will be times every day that we might disagree with someone else's opinion or behavior. As long as we remain accountable for our own words and behaviors, then we can't always control other people's actions. Sometimes you need to let things go and realize that one bad deed does not in turn deserve another. You've heard the expression; *"Two wrongs don't make a right"* and it's absolutely true. Just because someone does something you don't like, does not mean that retaliation is necessary. Be the bigger person and put an end to the ungodly ways of those around you.

When you conduct your life in an honest and upright fashion, you'll reap many of life's joyful surprises, mistakes and accidents that turn into blessings. No need for lying means total freedom to do more things you like; knowing you have other people's best interest at heart. Your life will be less stressful, because you can accomplish the tasks entrusted in you by family, friends, teachers, employers and strangers whom you have yet to meet.

Anthony Phillips

STEP FIVE

COMMUNICATION

The ability to talk about your feelings is a learned skill. Some people are fortunate to have parents who instill these skills within children at an early age. Others have poor communication skills themselves, making it difficult to teach to their children.

Good communicating is more than just saying how you feel. We all have thoughts, emotions, moods, opinions, morals, values and feelings that are different than anyone else's. How we are raised does determine a good half of how we learn to communicate. The other half is based on our individual personality and characteristics, plus the influences of our friends and society around us. Look in any direction for a confusing blend of messages. How do we know what is real or made up? How do we know who to believe?

All of the mixed-up values of society intertwine to create chaos. It's no wonder people are confused. Much of the confusion is due to a worldwide differing of views, caused by poor communicating.

What does that have to do with you? How does effectively communicating help to improve your self-esteem? Everyone must communicate their thoughts and ideas in order to have their interpersonal needs met. Many misunderstandings could be avoided if the two people involved are able to reach an agreement simply by communicating each of their needs to the other; thus reaching some compromise.

A person with high self-esteem is neither passive nor aggressive. They are simply assertive. They ask for what they need and they usually have more needs met because of their assertiveness.

There are two key concepts of communication. One is physical, while the other is verbal. Both of them can be used in sync to send a message. Here are the two main differences:

1) Physical Communications – This is your body language. Using facial expressions, hand signals, posture, gestures, crossing or uncrossing of legs and arms, stance or any part of your body to indicate approachability. With physical communication, it is important to relay the right

message in the best manner. Would an outside observer see you as approachable? Facial and bodily expressions are the first sign of whether or not you are approachable.

Do you...

- Smile or frown as someone talks to you?
- Sit or stand when someone offers a handshake?
- Hold your head up high during conversation?
- Look away or toward someone who speaks to you?
- Cross your arms in impatience, or make hand gestures to get your point across?
- Have relaxed or stiff posture?
- Keep an even or stressful expression?
- Laugh, cry or express emotions with your mannerisms?
- Have a negative or positive attitude?

Your physical demeanor is the body language you convey to outsiders. A person with a low self-esteem or lack of confidence might cower, slouch or act disinterested because they fear having a real conversation. The person might also seem bored, angry or stressed out. A person with a positive self-image will stand up tall, smile, hug or touch others during conversation and will have more enthusiasm than someone who is less assertive.

How many times have you changed your mind about approaching someone just because they had a negative expression on their face? Who knows, they may feel wonderful on the inside but the body language does not match their facial gestures. A person with crossed arms and crossed brows sends a message that says, "I don't want to be bothered!"

On the other hand, someone who displays a relaxed posture makes other people around them more comfortable, therefore creating an internally positive attitude for both parties. As they say, "A smile is contagious." No matter what has happened to you today or yesterday, try not to let your body language become misconstrued in the form of negative energy. It will contribute to a low self-esteem to remain grumpy.

2) Verbal Communications – What you say, the tone of voice you use, the words you choose and the ability to express your thoughts, ideas and opinions. Physical and verbal communications go hand-in-hand. Since none of us were born to be mind readers, the only way for humans to coexist with one another is to express our thoughts, values, motives and views with the words we choose.

Think about it.

Do you...

- Raise your voice and yell to get your message across, or do you speak softly?
- Say nothing at all, at a time when you should say the most?
- Speak up and say how you feel or do you bottle your feelings up inside until they become mountains?
- Use polite terms in front of friends and adults, or do you use foul and inappropriate language?
- Have a versatile vocabulary & understanding of the English language?

69

- Only speak when spoken to, or do you raise your voice and opinions during conversations?
- Use the appropriate tone of voice when speaking to others? Or do you use sarcastic, whining or demanding tones?

First, you must decide the impression you wish to portray to others. When you see yourself as being a valued contributor of the thoughts and ideas you have, you will learn to speak your mind in a tactful way that does not offend the people you communicate with. It takes practice.

On the path to improved confidence, you must learn to speak your mind appropriately using proper body language and facial expressions. Someone who is "reserved" is someone who holds back. They seem withdrawn, quiet and timid. It is a sign of weakness and insecurity. They are afraid of what someone else might think.

Weak people often swear, rant or yell, make lewd gestures as a means of communicating. They think that their message will be more effective, when in reality it can have the opposite effect.

On the contrary, a confident individual will speak with a professional, courteous tone and often smile a lot. Their body language and style will be inviting. People with a high self-esteem are more approachable and sure of themselves. Because they respect themselves, they also respect other people.

While no one is perfect, the golden rule (and one of the 10 commandments) is to do unto others as you would have them do unto you. That rule can apply to all of the words and actions you choose. Speak to another in rudeness and you will deserve the same, but treat another with respect and dignity and he will likely return the feeling.

"Let no corrupt communications proceed out of your mouth, but that which is good to the use of edifying, that it may minister grace unto the hearers."

~ Ephesians 4:29 ~

Another indication of a person who has a low self-esteem is the kind who says nothing at all. They are the type of individual who displays very little expression or emotion. It may be the opposite extreme of the people who yell, swear, act violently or who act inappropriately and loudly. These types of people are withdrawn. Their anger and lack of confidence is internal.

Bottling up feelings can lead to resentment, anger and frustration. If you are afraid to speak your mind because of a fear of how someone else might react, it is a sign of poor communication. Not speaking your mind can backlash just as easily as saying the wrong thing. It leads to misunderstandings between two people. It also allows people to walk all over you, when they realize that you're not willing to stand up for your own values.

Part of effective communications is to set boundaries. God is in charge and you need to trust him to steer you in the right direction. When you allow people to influence you without speaking your mind, bad things can happen. Like this story:

Easy-going Elixis was a nice girl who lived in the suburbs of a big city. Her mother and stepfather took her to church nearly every week. She was a gifted student, who rarely got into trouble. Elixis's mild-mannered nature was passive. She preferred to be a follower, more so than a leader.

Of particular enjoyment were the afternoons with her best friend in the whole world, Tori. Tori and Elixis were quite inseparable. Undeniably, Tori was the leader. Both of them belonged to a circle of friends who liked to hang out together and have slumber parties, hangouts at the mall's arcade area and sometimes the movie cinema.

Elixis didn't mind going along with Tori's ideas. They were always fun. Besides, she was a little shy and not yet confident in her appearance. Elixis's mother wouldn't let her wear any makeup like the other girls her age, which made her self-conscious. Inside, she wished she could do it anyway. Sometimes Elixis wondered how she would ever fit in if it weren't for Tori, who was louder and a little more rebellious.

Anthony Phillips

Toward the end of their sophomore year in high school, Tori found a couple of new friends for them to hang out with. Elixis, who was always eager to please, went along with it, despite rumors that the two girls were both known to be unruly party-goers. They invited the bosom buddies to a party the next weekend. Tori accepted on behalf of both of them, even though Elixis seemed a little hesitant. She didn't speak up.

Elixis was taught never to lie to her parents, so instead she didn't tell them. She was too afraid to ask for permission to go. Her communication to her parents was just that she was spending the night at Tori's house. Elixis "left out" the part that the girls were going to a party.

After being dropped off at Tori's house, the two girls prepared for their grand evening. Tori talked Elixis into letting her put makeup on. She also picked out an outfit for her friend to wear. "Here", Tori said as she dropped the mini skirt and tank top in her lap. "Tonight we must look cool. The juniors invited us to their party."

Elixis hated how deceitful she felt as she let Tori put the makeup on her face. She knew her mom would disapprove. Yet, Elixis went along with it, because she

74

didn't want her longtime friend not to like her. Elixis lacked the confidence to confront Tori with her true feelings. Losing her friendship would be unthinkable.

The girls arrived at the party. The host greeted both of them with a beer in hand. "Want one?" asked the party girl. Tori grabbed one, but Elixis held back.

The girl then trotted off to mingle. Tori pulled Elixis aside. "What's wrong with you? This is our chance to hang with the cool crowd. Aren't you down for that?"

"I'm just going to wait a bit", cringed Elixis. Inside, she wished she could just go home. That would surely not look good though.

Later in the evening, people became drunker and drunker. More teenagers streamed in through the front door. Elixis faked drinking by holding a bottle of beer most of the evening. She took one sip and nearly gagged. Secretly, she dumped it slowly down the sink to make it look like she had been drinking.

"C'mon – road trip!" yelled someone. Tori pulled Elixis's arm and guided her to a car. Two boys and another girl were with them. "We're making a beer run"; said the driver.

As Elixis sat in the backseat, she wished she had the nerve to speak up. She had an uncomfortable feeling with these strangers and was increasingly more and more irritated with Tori's behavior and quest for popularity.

They all stopped at a small convenience store. The guy driving had a fake I.D. He came out of the store with two 12-packs and a big paper bag with a jug sticking out. On the return trip to the party, the kids were laughing and listening to music loud. The driver took a corner erratically and then ran a red light. There was a cop at the right corner of the intersection.

Needless to say, the blue lights appeared behind the party animals' car within a few seconds. The cop asked for the I.D. and insurance. He asked the boy to step out of the car for a sobriety test while pointing the flashlight at everyone else in the car. Elixis was petrified.

"Is there anyone in this car who is over 18?" asked the policeman. "Or for that matter, is there anyone here with a driver's license?" The other boy raised his hand.

"You're all in big trouble. The law says anyone under 21 is a minor and that makes drinking illegal", said the stern policeman. "Everyone in this car is going to the station right now."

At that point, Elixis's parent's faces popped into her head. All because she failed to speak up, the whole evening turned into a nightmare. Her fear and failure to say how she felt had caused her to get in trouble. At the station, she really felt like a criminal. The police officer made Elixis call her parents. It was the worst feeling in the world to call and hear her stepfather say, "We'll be right there"; in a mad tone of voice. The police officer told her parents the whole story; although she had not drank like the others.

Based on the fact that she was merely in the backseat, the officer let her go with only a brief probation time to serve. She hung her head as her stepfather scolded her all the way home. Her mom was mostly disappointed because she felt that Elixis's trustworthiness had been betrayed.

All of this could have been avoided, had Elixis been forthright and solid with her personal values. Her failure to speak her mind because of a fear of being liked was the reason for her trouble. All she had to do was incorporate the positive self-esteem principles with assertiveness, poise and confidence. Communication is necessary to do this.

Communication with parents, friends, teachers, family, boyfriends and girlfriends is necessary in order to maintain good relationships. *Not saying anything can be just as bad as saying the wrong thing.*

Free yourself from these communication busters and feel empowered:

- Fear – of anyone's feelings being hurt, letting go of pride or fear of failure.
- Clamming up – an unwillingness to face confrontation.
- Avoidance – instead of facing a challenge head-on you think it best to run away.
- Misunderstanding – Make sure both people thoroughly know all of the details, like: who, where, what and why before either has a chance to realize inaccuracies.
- Bending the truth – People do this to avoid telling the whole story.
- Quarrels – Confrontation can be avoided by discussing both sides.
- Not listening – Some people talk, while others listen. The ratio should be half and half. If

someone does more talking than listening, it can lead to miscommunications.

To incorporate these concepts of communication into your daily living – start with a simple changing of your facial expressions and choice of words that you use. Keep a positive frame of mind (including that beautiful smile) with an inviting disposition. When you speak to others, give concrete examples and explanations of your expectations. Remember that no one can read your mind, nor do you want them to.

Once you become better at communicating, it will positively change your level of confidence. Saying out loud to others how you feel is enlightening, like a feeling of freedom; freedom from worry about what other people think. You have your own mind, so speak it!

Anthony Phillips

STEP SIX

MENTORING

We all have someone we look up to. It could be an older brother or sister, cousin or close friend. Often we look up to people who are older than we are, because they have more experience and worldly knowledge. Whether that person is a school pal who's the same age, or maybe a young adult you know – there could be someone you confide in who provides you with motivating guidance.

Not everyone has the luxury of a close mentor. A mentor is someone who encourages, educates, guides and invests time into helping another person to reach his or her goals. Those can be any combination of personal, financial or academic goals that the young person desires. Consider it much like a teacher and student, even if the teacher is just a classmate.

Think of a person whom you know to be a leader; someone like the Quarterback of the high school football team, the captain of the cheering squad, the editor of the school newspaper or the class president. These kids possess proven leadership ability. They are able to assemble a "team" and to guide that team to make the best motions toward success. Leaders have plans and are quick to think on their feet. Leaders make on-the-spot decisions without stuttering or questioning their own abilities. They just do it.

You may have heard of programs that already have the mentor mentality. A well-known "Big Brother" program is alive in many cities. The Big Brother or Big Sister is a person who spends time with youth and assist with helping them reach their potential. Big Brothers or Sisters can spend as much time as they like, from once a week, an afternoon or every day with the youth.

Many of the young kids are latchkey children who come home from school and then have to fend for themselves. Their parents are often single mothers (sometimes Dads) who work during the day and are not able to take time off from working to stay home with their kids. The kids are frequently lonely, depressed or troublemakers. The intention of the mentor is to turn these kids' lives around for the better.

How does a mentor turn these kids' lives around? They care about them. They want to spend time with them to help them. Picture it like this – it's kind of like hanging out with a good pal, except one who is a good influence and who will teach you life's lessons while you're hanging out together.

Sometimes kids have a hard time talking to their parents about tough topics. Subjects like sex, drugs, alcohol, nicotine or personal issues are left out during dinner table conversation. So, the mentor serves as harbor for the student to trust. He or she becomes a sounding board for the child to talk about issues that might be uncomfortable to talk about with a parent or legal guardian.

The mentor's job is to give the best advice possible. They do this by earning trust and spending time with the youth each week. It's a win-win for both, because the child learns to trust and listen to an older kid without compromising "coolness" and without having to worry about punishment by a parent.

The mentor helps to teach the child wrong from right without judging or belittling them. Meanwhile, they both learn valuable skills on leadership and life's lessons. Some mentors take their students to organized activities like: sports; band; tae-kwon do classes; dance or other events. Others become the student's tutor to assist with difficult homework assignments.

Whenever people are put in a position of leadership, there is an instant boost to their level of confidence. A leader is someone that people look up to. Therefore, mentors almost always possess a high self-esteem. And what a great gift to have a positive self worth at such an early age. Mentors always seem to know what they're doing, where they're going and how to handle a situation. Maybe it's just an optical illusion, but certainly those skills are within all of us. You may not think that you could be a mentor to someone else if you have a low evaluation of your own capabilities.

Now is the best time to give it a try... If you know a kid who looks up to you, do you set a good example to him? Do you spend time with him? Do you offer words of encouragement or advice? Become a mentor to a child or even a close friend of the same age. Doing this will not only help to improve your own self esteem, it will make someone else's life blessed because of it.

You could become a mentor to someone else, _and_ have your own mentor. Define your personal goals and think about what you do or don't want to do. Perhaps you have unique talents that you wish to cultivate. Let's say you want to become a better basketball player. It would be great to find a mentor who is better than you. That person will teach you new dribbling tricks, passing, shooting, etc. However, you may already be a pretty decent basketball player yourself and the mentor will only help you to become better, therefore, you could become a mentor to younger kids who may need _you_. You could volunteer at a basketball camp or become a coach for the elementary grade kids. Of course, basketball is just an illustration here to show you how mentoring is beneficial to you and to the people you help.

Let's create a "Mentor Wish List"

If you could have the perfect mentor for yourself, what qualities would you most desire?

- What would he or she be able to do for you?
- Would your mentor provide you with information or skills you need to be successful?

- Would your mentor give you a list of books to read that would help you move closer toward your goals?
- Do you want advice from your mentor on how to dress, speak or behave?
- Is your mentor there to encourage you?

In most cases, a mentor would not be able to drop everything and rush to your aid. Hopefully, they will have given you the advice that you need along the way so that you can make rational decisions on your own. That is exactly why a mentor is such a good influence on a youth's self-esteem. In case you are faced with a crisis, you will have learned the skills to be able to deal with it on your own.

Relying on your faith in God is part of dealing with and facing situations on your own. He is always your mentor, much more so than any human. If you listen, he will send those perfect people in your life that can guide you, help you and lead you down your chosen journey.

"... fear not, for I am with you; be not dismayed,
for I am your God; I will strengthen you, I will help you,
I will uphold you with my righteous right hand."
~ Isaiah 41:10 ~

When you let God guide you, you will not fail! Be a mentor to someone else. Be a mentor to yourself! Let God guide you by following these steps:

1) Pray and ask God to show you your purpose; then ask him to guide you through life and give you the needed wisdom to full it.

We all have a God given purpose, but many people go through life without ever knowing why they exist. Most tend to live a life of regret and sorrow and if you took a survey, you would probably find that many failed to seek Gods guidance for their purpose in life.

2) Think about what you want to accomplish. Make a list called – "EVERTHING I WANT TO DO DURING MY TIME HERE ON EARTH."

This should be a fun list. Allocate at least two or three notebook pages and just write down a whole bunch of things (within your lifetime or within the next 5 years, whatever you like!) – skydiving; visiting Italy; becoming a doctor; finding the soul mate of your dreams; living in a big beautiful condo in the Bahamas; or all the wishes of your own heart's desire. Keep this list in your nightstand or readily available. Then make it a goal to cross as many things off the list as you can!

3) *Refer to the list of qualities that you want in a mentor and learn to develop them for you. You can find out what works and doesn't work for those so called idols you aspire to be like.*

Many teenagers idolize celebrities and think of them as mentors. Unfortunately, some of the celebrities do not have the highest morals and values. There are many that do, but be careful who you choose to idolize or place on a pedestal. Ask yourself if those celebrities whom you admire do anything to contribute to the better good of society, or do they have false values of materialistic and ungodly ways? It would be better to fill your mind with spiritually-fulfilling people to admire. Think of great authors, poets, ministers or athletes who have overcome injuries and great adversities; think of actors who have gone on to become great governors or presidents and think of divas who adopt misfortunate children from poor countries. These types of celebrities do something to set a good example for everyone. Don't follow the examples of those who are always in the tabloids for bad behavior. Some are in and out of rehab clinics and have been married and divorced multiple times. Life does not have to be filled with such drama. Watch documentaries of successful people and listen to what they have to say. What it all boils down to is this – *do you really want people to remember you for the good in the world you have done, or will they only think of the bad?* Leave a legacy that is fitting for your time here on earth.

4) *Ask people. What do other people think about your ideas? Maybe they have better suggestions.*

If so, try them. If not, don't worry. You can keep trying until you find a solution that works for you.

Above all else, be true to yourself. Make certain that the image, ideas, vocabulary and flavor that you have is your own authentic true you, not how you "think you should be" or how others expect you to be.

With or without a mentor, you can still become a mentor to others through the concepts and talents that you have unlike anyone else's. When you use those ideas and skills to help someone else, the good you do will leave a legacy in the mind of those you help. It will also lead to good things happening for you.

STEP SEVEN

SELF EXPECTANCY

Self-expectancy involves a great deal of effort, every day. In a society of so much negativity, it can be hard not to succumb to the concepts of a large population who believe that only bad things lie ahead. If you listen to the media or the buzz around school – everywhere around you are people struggling, complaining, unhappy and frustrated.

While you can be compassionate to the problems of others, you must never fall into their trap. They want people to believe that things are bad and only getting worse. They live their lives in fear. Fear leads to bad things and false ideals.

If you think something bad is about to happen, it probably will. Learning to think positively is an acquired skill. It takes practice. It takes effort. But this is also a large part in your effort to improve your self-esteem. Here's something many people don't understand. If you expect the worst, you will be more likely to get the worst. If you expect the best, mostly likely you will get the best if that's what you believe will happen. Sure, sometimes you may be faced with an occasional disappointment.

You deserve the best, so why not expect it? Don't let other people's jaded ways of thinking bring you down.

Throughout history, people have believed that the world is coming to an end in only a few years. Still now, millions fear that the world is coming to an end soon. Yet every single time, the world stays put despite the predictions.

Y2K is a great example. If you don't remember Y2K, it happened when the new millennium changed in the year 2000. You may have been too young to remember. No one truly knows if or when it will take place, if at all. There is no reason you can't live your best life now, without worry of things standing in your way. You can acknowledge the current events and hot news topics, but try not to become sucked in by the fear they try to implant in people.

Having a positive self-esteem means having the knowledge that no matter what happens, you will prevail. You will come out on top. You will be victorious.

Challenges will come and will sometimes seem like obstacles. They are put there to see how bad you want it. If good things were easy to acquire, then everyone would have nothing but good things. Good things take effort. Many of today's most attractive, successful, wealthiest stars were once failures. Their power to continue positive thoughts and actions allowed them to keep on going until they finally achieved their goals. Some rather famous celebrities came from dirt poor families in the streets of poor urban neighborhoods. Others suffered a great loss and went on to beat the odds. Not everyone is born into celebrity status – in fact, hardly any. Most famous people have worked hard to achieve their success.

What they all have in common is

SELF-EXPANTANCY.

They knew deep down that they were good enough, talented enough and they had a support system of family and mentors. If you have a low self-esteem, you might think that you're not good enough. Look in the mirror and ask yourself, *why not me?* If famous people can do it, you can too. Pay no mind to people who say that you can't do something that is a goal of yours to achieve. It is your goal, so who has a right to stand in your way?

You may have heard the word tenacious (or tenacity) before. It's a Latin adjective meaning to hold firmly to something; to persist in existence or in a course of action.

te·na·cious ◀ᵢ)   \ti-nay-shess\

To be tenacious means to pursue something fiercely and with determination. You know it will happen and expect it to happen. Self-expectancy is a tenacious quality to have.

To put a modern example of people who have overcome great obstacles to become great, look at Usher. Usher began his singing career when he was only 10 years old. His family moved several times and had been rejected over four times by several different record labels. Yet, he never thought about giving up altogether, ever. He was steadfast in his determination to be a singer. Usher's mother told him that he had to make a decision about his music career because their family funds were running low due to all his efforts with one producer after another. Of course, we all know Usher decided to stick it out and now the rest is history – he has sold over 35 million albums and has won five Grammy Awards.

Another contemporary example of positive self-expectancy is the Destiny's Child diva herself, Beyonce. She had performed in over four different singing groups since the third grade, then when she turned 14, her mom and dad split up. They were considering a divorce. Since Beyonce's father was also her manager, she chose to live with him so that she could continue to pursue her music career. Beyonce's mother asked her if she wanted to live a "normal" life instead, meaning to come back home with her and attend public schools. For Beyonce, this crossroads could have changed her destiny as a singer. She decided to stay with her father.

Beyonce's Dad fired all of her childhood friends and Beyonce had to live her life out of a suitcase for a few difficult years. She made new friends. Her parents eventually reconciled. Throughout her ordeals, Beyonce continued to believe in her own skills and talents.

The moral of these celebrity examples is that you have to take a risk in order to be successful. You have to have firm belief in your dreams and know that they will happen if you just persevere. Nothing of value comes easy.

Everything good in life requires commitment and a positive attitude. Your life can be whatever you want it to be. To increase your self-expectancy, you must capitalize on the things that you do well. In another chapter, we talked about determining those things you do best. Start by thinking of things that people tell you you're good at, or things you enjoy doing. What are you passionate about?

By incorporating a positive attitude and a feeling of self-expectancy, you will develop a winning attitude. You will become more daring and ready to take a chance, because you will expect to be successful.

We all face the pressures and expectations of others on a daily basis. People put pressure on us to perform. They expect us to be on time. They expect us to do what is asked of us. They expect us to honor our commitments. They expect good grades. Your success is measured by others, not by you.

When you start to evaluate your own expectations, you will realize that true success is best spent in the minutes that bring you closer to your goals. But you are capable of going beyond what people see in you and becoming better by your own heart's desire.

For example, many teens spend hours in front of the TV or sitting around. "I'm bored," they say to their parents. Their parents expect no more from them than to just sit there and do nothing, so that is what they do. Take some initiative to do something on your own. Pick up a hobby or some positive, like-minded friends. Use your imagination and think of something fun or different to do. Expect better for yourself than what you have been introduced to. Likewise, don't set too high of expectations on others. It will usually lead to letdowns and disappointments. There are ways you can increase your self-expectancy, next time you feel the weight of the world is on your shoulders.

USE THESE 10 SELF-EXPECTANCY STRATEGIES:

1) Expect to win. Always. Someone has to win and someone has to lose, so why shouldn't you be the winner?

2) Be optimistic. Always believe in yourself.

3) Be tenacious and never give up on anything you truly want, no matter how unbelievable or unattainable it may seem to you right now.

4) Overcome problems by treating them as opportunities to do better, learn something or simply as bumps in the road. Never let problems interfere with your main mission.

5) Stop complaining. Things will go better for you if you don't get caught up in the negativity that has infested the minds of the majority of people.

6) Get excited, passionate and enthusiastic about your own dreams. If you're just 'ho-hum' about it and 'hope that it might happen one day'; that's not the right attitude to take. You should know and be positive that it will be forthcoming.

7) Don't criticize others. Instead, offer helpful advice. Who are you to rain on anybody's parade?

8) Ask for help when you need it. Don't be too proud or macho to turn down help when it is offered. If you expect others to take advantage of you, they will. If you expect to be treated with respect, loyalty and admiration, they will.

9) Praise others. Give credit where it is due.

10) Don't ever give up on yourself. Continue to set your sights on what you want and strive to meet those achievements.

Remember that a large part of increasing your self-esteem is by having positive thoughts about the wonderful person you are, the good things to come and a confidence in your abilities. You will become a winner with everything you do. Everybody loves to be a winner. Self-expectancy is the secret to becoming a winner.

CONCLUSION

BELIEVE IN YOURSELF

"It's not who you are that holds you back,
it's who you think you're not."
~ Author Unknown ~

The seven steps to positive self-esteem can all be done by believing in yourself and having confidence in your abilities. It is the core of who we become, in the early crucial stages of development; such as you are experiencing as a teenager moving toward the fascinating stage of adulthood.

Learn to make decisions based on your own intuition and experiences. If you don't have your own opinion and always have to ask someone else what to do, then you'll have a hard time ever becoming successful. Rely on you and only you. Don't let other people make decisions for you because they may not always have your best interest at heart.

The bottom line is – START CARING! Care about yourself and dare to become the person you were born to be. Everyone is put on this planet for a specific reason, yet many people fail to discover what that reason may be because they are too busy getting wrapped up in self-pity.

If you just feel 'blah' all the time, don't try very hard at school, fail to do your chores and basically become lazy, then you will likely hold that same work ethic later on. It could take you half your life to finally find a great career and the spouse of your dreams. Then one day you will wake up and say, "Why did I waste half my life by doing nothing with it?"

Older people do this, not just young people. A 70-year old woman said, "I wish I had gotten married and had a family, but I was one of those career women who worked at the TV station. For my era, it was considered brave for a woman to choose her career. But now I think it would have been nice to have both, because I am all alone with no one to share the end of my years with."

Don't ever become one of those people who regret things later on in life. When you feel strongly compelled to do something that you feel is right, do it. Don't second guess your own feelings because often your intuition and instinct will lead you in the right direction.

Believe it when it is there. It goes for both good and bad emotions – if you feel like you shouldn't do something, it could be your inner guidance mechanism kicking in to say "Whoa!" so don't go there. However, if you have a once-in-a lifetime opportunity come along and you make an excuse or find a reason not to trust it, then you may miss out on your true chance to grab success.

It doesn't mean the chance won't come again one day. Our own new president, Mr. Obama admitted to being "a goof-off" in high school. As we know, he aspired for more and eventually went on to graduate from two Ivy League universities, teach constitutional law and ultimately be elected into office. He had dreamed of being in the NBA, like many kids his age… but instead of getting stuck at a standstill when that dream did not happen, President Obama found new goals to achieve.

"… in school, I didn't push myself very hard," explained the now president. "At some point, you've got to internalize the idea that nobody should have higher expectations for you than you. Find out what excites you. Work on something that makes you feel good to get up in the morning." He ended the speech with; "Believe in yourself – because we believe in you."

Your goals may change many times throughout your life, which is perfectly okay. Go with the flow and let your inner gut guide you toward success and happiness. Trust it and believe it. **All you need is you!**

BELIEVE IN YOURSELF WITH THESE 10 TECHNIQUES:

1) Set realistic expectations. Work toward them, like a ladder until you reach the pinnacle. Picture yourself running toward them. Make those strides in steps, as if you are trying to reach a finish line every week, except each time trying to break a record that you beat before.

2) Realize failures and use them as leverage to better yourself, rather than giving up or getting angry. Sometimes the reason for a failure is actually for a better cause that you will not discover right away.

3) Reward yourself when you meet goals. Give yourself time to enjoy the outcomes. Relish in the

successes and victories you achieve. It will build your confidence.

4) Never listen to naysayers who say you can't do something. If you believe them, then it makes them right.

5) If someone loves you, you should love them back unconditionally. It will teach you how to open your eyes, heart and soul to the tremendous gift of love. Make every minute count and be happy together. It also helps your self-esteem to give and receive love.

6) Don't let anyone tear you down just to make themselves look better or convince you that you are any less than you are. Often people do this just to cover up their own low self-esteem and it is a way to make themselves feel better. Brush it off and let it go.

7) Sit up straight, hold your head up and walk with poise and confidence. Why? Because you have every right to. You are awesome. You were put on this earth for a purpose and you matter to someone, or many people.

8) Say this repeatedly out loud or to yourself every day, "I deserve the best that life has in store for me. I deserve to have a life of happiness and success." Knowing you deserve good things is what believing in yourself is all about. Many people – especially teens – are taught to think that they don't deserve things. This is false. Everyone deserves the best that life has to offer.

9) Even if you don't have any money, you can give of your time and energy to others. The good deeds you do will make others happy, which in turn makes you feel good and creates a positive chain of events. It will also give you self respect to know that you are doing your part to contribute meaningfully to individuals or organizations that need you.

10) Believe in God's presence watching over you. He wants you to succeed just as much as you do. Remember that things happen for a reason and sometimes when it seems like just good luck, it's actually just the course of events that you are meant to follow. Life tests like lost loves, pain, grief, or bad choices with disastrous outcomes are as much a part of the plan as the positive

things. Without them, life would be too smooth. It would be safe, dull and comfortable but truly meaningless. Humans are meant to live life and experience a wide range of emotions, activities, events and people in order to feel fulfilled by the time they hopefully reach "a mature age". Next time things don't go as planned, realize you are on God's plan and just go with it.

> *"He who comes to God must believe that He is, and that He is a rewarder of those who seek Him."*
> **~ Hebrews 11:6 ~**

If you learned a lot from the 7 Steps to Positive Self-Esteem, then you begin to incorporate small, yet profound changes into your daily life. Soon you will begin to see how your life circumstances *can* and *will* improve. There is a direct link between your willingness to take action and between happiness for your personal and financial success. These are journeys. There is never a dead end unless you choose to stay stuck in a rut.

The worst beatings we take are those that we inflict upon ourselves. Sometimes people make a mistake and give up before the referee blows the whistle. It can lead to depression – a dreary and dark hole that leads to tears, anger, frustration and many other negative emotions.

Life can be full of questions. But where are the answers? The answers are just waiting to be found. You can talk to God and ask him for the answers. He will always give them to you if you are open to receiving them, rather than trying to do things your own way.

Your self-esteem is a foundation of your character and personality. It is your view on how you see yourself and your perception of the outside world.

When you wake up in the morning, try to get a clear picture in your mind of your self-image. Take it day by day. What can you accomplish today? What good can you do for yourself and for others? Are you happy with yourself today?

A great place to begin is with your very own private journal. Journaling is a way to discover who you are and where you want to go. You will begin to uncover emotions, deep-rooted fears, joys, victories and it will help you to get to know yourself and God. Write down positive affirmations on post-it-notes and stick them to a mirror. Find pictures and inspirational quotes to put inside your locker.

By doing things like these, you will soon realize what a great person you are. You were born for a reason, whether you think so or not. There are no "accidents" or coincidences. God has a master plan.

Life is complex and multidimensional. All aspects of your personality and decision-making will come into play during your daily interactions with people. You won't wake up and have every situation happen exactly as planned. However, you should be able to easily apply these great ideas to gain more control over your own level of personal gratification.

"People often say that this or that person has not yet found himself. But the self is not something one finds, it is something one creates."
~ Thomas Szasz – 1973 ~